STOP COUNTING YOUR NEIGHBOR'S PETUNIAS

Finding Joy In Your Own Backyard

WORKBOOK

TEMPEST MERIWETHER

Meriwether, T. (2025). *Stop Counting Your Neighbor's Petunias: Workbook* T. Meriwether; T. Scott, TLScott Publishing

ISBN 979-8-9856532-3-6

CHAPTER

TABLE OF CONTENTS

Chapter 1

WHEN THE WORLD FORCES YOU TO COMPARE

Comparison. We all do it at some point. It is how we measure ourselves against everyone else and decide if we are worthy. Does she have a better body? Is their spouse more loving? Do they have more money? Are they living "better" lives than me? Comparison is a part of our social wiring as humans. From the time we are born we are compared to others and continue throughout the life span. While it may be natural, if left unchecked, it can wreak havoc on our overall well-being.

DIGGING DEEPER

Write your answers to the following journaling prompts.

Exploring Roots of Comparison
What areas of my life do I most often compare myself to others, and how do societal or cultural standards influence these comparisons?

Impact of Comparison
How does comparison impact my mental and emotional well-being, and what unique aspects of my journey do I tend to overlook?

Cultivating Self-Acceptance
What affirmations can I create to counteract the negative effects of comparison and cultivate self-acceptance?

Moving Forward

What boundaries can I set and practices can I adopt to minimize triggers for unhealthy comparison and foster self-compassion?

_____

_____

_____

_____

_____

_____

_____

_____

_____

_____

_____

_____

_____

_____

_____

_____

_____

Chapter 2

UNPLUGGING FROM THE GAME

The game of comparison is a never-ending game that no one ever really wins. The best way to win the game is to unplug from it all together and focus your energy on things that give you joy rather than sap it away. There will always be something new to compare. Someone has a nicer car, a bigger house, takes more extravagant vacations, or a more loving spouse. In order to unplug from the game, it is better to focus on connection rather than comparison.

DIGGING DEEPER:

Write your answers to the following journaling prompts.

Focusing on Connection

How can I celebrate the successes of others without comparing them to my own life, and what does that look like in practice?

Who in my life do I feel most connected to, and how can I intentionally nurture that relationship this week?

Finding Joy

How can I redirect the energy I spend comparing myself to others into activities that bring me joy, fulfillment, or creativity?

Taking Action

What boundaries can I set to reduce exposure to comparison triggers this week (e.g., limiting social media, avoiding certain conversations)?

_____

_____

_____

_____

_____

_____

_____

_____

_____

_____

_____

_____

_____

_____

_____

_____

_____

_____

_____

Chapter 3

IF GOD IS IN THE NEIGHBORHOOD

In the South, there is a common saying that if God is blessing your neighbor, it means He is in the neighborhood. This statement is problematic because, one, we are likely ignoring what we are already blessed with, and two, we are turning other people's blessings into being about us when God's timetable for you and other people are completely different. Envy really does have a way of "rotting our bones." It steals our joy and makes us not be able to enjoy the blessings of others. Envy makes us pay too much attention to what is going on in our neighbor's house instead of our own.

DIGGING DEEPER:
Write your answers to the following journaling prompts.

Reflecting on Envy
What are three areas of my life where I often feel envious, and how does envy affect my thoughts or relationships?

Focusing on Gratitude
What are three blessings or successes in my life that I may overlook, and how can I focus on celebrating them?

Changing Perspective

How can I celebrate the successes of others without feeling like it diminishes my own journey?

How can I redirect the energy spent on envy to improve or appreciate aspects of my own life?

_____

_____

_____

_____

_____

_____

_____

_____

_____

_____

_____

_____

_____

_____

Chapter 4

LIVING IN THE SOCIAL MEDIA ERA - PART 1

Many of us are aware that social media can fuel comparison, envy, and consumerism. Yet, we often dismiss its impact on us. Studies have linked social media to a variety of negative mental health outcomes, but many can't stop scrolling. Regaining control over social media is crucial for enhancing happiness and reducing comparison.

DIGGING DEEPER
Write your answers to the following journaling prompts.

Reflecting on the Impact of Social Media
How do I feel after scrolling through social media? Do I notice any patterns of comparison, envy, or other negative emotions?

Examining Current Social Media Habits
How much time do I spend on social media each day? How often do I check it during idle moments? Do I follow, or engage with content that doesn't align with values or well-being?

Establishing Healthier Boundaries
What are some specific boundaries I can set to limit my social media usage (e.g., time limits, designated no-phone times)?

Reclaiming Joy and Focus

How can I remind myself that social media is a curated highlight reel, and how might reducing my use of it improve my mental and emotional well-being?

_____

_____

_____

_____

_____

_____

_____

_____

_____

_____

_____

_____

_____

_____

_____

Chapter 4

LIVING IN THE SOCIAL MEDIA ERA - PART 2

Are you someone who does the opposite on social media? Is social media a place where you are constantly looking down on others? This is still a form of comparison. You may be thinking that because you don't post as much and because you are the cynical type who believes everyone is lying, you aren't getting caught in the trap. However, if you're still scrolling for hours, guess what? You are just as trapped as everyone else. Comparing yourself to others in a way that makes you superior is just as unhealthy of a practice as the reverse. It pulls us away from connection with others instead of toward it.

DIGGING DEEPER
Write your answers to the following journaling prompts.

Reflecting on Superior Comparison
What situations, people, or posts make me feel superior on social media, and how do these judgments and assumptions affect my view of others and my ability to connect authentically?

Shifting Toward Connection
How can I remind myself that everyone's life is complex, even if it doesn't align with my values or perspective?

What are some ways I can shift from judgment to empathy when scrolling through social media?

Taking Action Toward Intentional Connection

How can I use social media more intentionally to foster connection rather than disconnection?

Chapter 5

UNREALISTIC EXPECTATIONS

Many disappointments in life come from unmet expectations. We craft narratives about how we want things to unfold and how others should behave, hoping everyone will follow our script. To find greater happiness, we must recognize our expectations, evaluate their realism, adjust when needed, and communicate them clearly, all while remembering that we can only control ourselves.

DIGGING DEEPER:

Write your answers to the following journaling prompts.

Reflecting on Expectations for Yourself

What are some expectations I have for myself in different areas of life (e.g., career, personal growth, relationships)?

Are there any expectations I have for myself that I can let go of, as they may be too rigid or unrealistic?

Reflecting on Expectations of Others

What expectations do I have of the people around me, and are they reasonable given their abilities, circumstances, and what I know about them?

Letting Go and Adjusting Expectations

How can I adjust my expectations to align with the reality of what the person is capable of or willing to offer?

\
\
\
\
\
\
\
\
\
\
\
\
\
\
\
\
\
\

Chapter 6

WHAT WE THINK IS TRUE VS. TRUE REALITY - PART 1

The brain has 20,000 to 50,000 thoughts a day, and most are the same ones we've had for years. Many of these thoughts are based on inaccuracies or incomplete information. Recognizing that our thoughts aren't always facts is key to managing life's challenges and finding joy.

DIGGING DEEPER

Write your answers to the following journaling prompts.

Tracking and Reflecting on Your Thoughts

What recurring thoughts or self-talk did I notice today, and were they based on facts, assumptions, or past experiences?

Questioning the Accuracy of Your Thoughts

How can I challenge a negative or recurring thought by asking, "Is this true, and what evidence supports or challenges it?"

Shifting the Narrative

What would be a more balanced or positive thought to replace this one with?

Reflection on Effectiveness

After reflecting on my thoughts, how do I feel now? Has my mindset shifted in a positive direction?

Chapter 6

WHAT WE THINK IS TRUE VS. TRUE REALITY - PART 2

Sometimes, what we think we want is something external, but we're actually seeking a deeper feeling. When you identify the true feeling behind your desires, you gain clarity on your needs and can find better ways to meet them.

DIGGING DEEPER

Write your answers to the following journaling prompts.

Reflecting on Your Desires

What is a goal I'm pursuing, and what specific feeling am I hoping it will bring me?

Exploring the Underlying Feeling

What deeper emotion am I truly seeking, and are there other ways to experience it beyond achieving my specific goal?

Have I experienced this feeling in the past without having the exact thing I think I need? How can I tap into that feeling again?

Finding Present Alternatives

What are some things I can do right now, today, to experience the feeling I'm hoping to achieve?

Chapter 7

SHIFT YOUR MINDSET

This book is a helpful tool to create a fulfilling life, but the techniques only work if they are used. Shifting your mindset and behavior is key to building the life you want, and it takes awareness and practice. Dwelling on the past often leads to depression, while worrying about the future causes anxiety.

DIGGING DEEPER
Write your answers to the following journaling prompts.

Reflecting on Your Thoughts
Do I spend more time thinking about the past or worrying about the future, and how do these thoughts typically make me feel?

When I'm focusing on the present moment, how does that make me feel differently (e.g., more grounded, calm, engaged)?

Shifting Toward the Present
What activities or practices help me stay present and in the moment? How can I incorporate more of these into my day?

What's one small step I can take today to practice staying present and engaged with my current experience?

Chapter 8

LOCUS OF CONTROL

Do you feel like your life is controlled by your own actions or by external factors? Your locus of control refers to where you believe that control comes from—within yourself or from outside influences. People with an internal locus of control believe they shape their own lives, while those with an external locus believe circumstances control them. Guess which mindset leads to more success? Those who believe they have the power to influence their own outcomes.

DIGGING DEEPER

Write your answers to the following journaling prompts.

Reflecting on Your Locus of Control

Do I feel like I am in control of my life, or do I often feel like circumstances or external factors are controlling me?

When things go well in my life, do I attribute that success to my own efforts, or do I credit luck, timing, or other people?

Finding Your Power

How can I shift my mindset to focus on the things I can control rather than the things I cannot?

What specific actions can I take to influence my outcomes or create positive change in my life?

Chapter 9

THE ILLUSION OF LACK

Whether we struggle with envy and comparison often depends on our mindset of scarcity versus abundance. Those who believe there's a limited amount of everything and feel they must fight for it have a very different experience from those who trust there's enough and that what's meant for them will come. Living with a scarcity mindset keeps you in survival mode, making it harder to escape envy and comparison and disconnecting you from others.

DIGGING DEEPER

Write your answers to the following journaling prompts.

Reflecting on Areas of Scarcity

In which areas of my life do I struggle with scarcity, and where do I feel a sense of abundance?

How does a scarcity mindset shape your thoughts, behaviors, and relationships, and what fears or beliefs might be driving this perception?

Shifting from Scarcity to Abundance

What steps can I take to create more abundance in areas where I feel lacking? What actions can I focus on that will reinforce an abundance mindset?

Strengthening the Abundance Mindset

What daily practices or affirmations can I use to cultivate a mindset of abundance in areas that feel scarce?

_____

_____

_____

_____

_____

_____

_____

_____

_____

_____

_____

_____

_____

_____

_____

_____

_____

Chapter 10

THE HEDONIC TREADMILL

The hedonic treadmill describes our tendency to adapt to new experiences and return to a baseline level of happiness. For example, buying a new car or getting married may bring temporary excitement, but eventually, we revert to our usual happiness level. This leads us to chase more, thinking each new acquisition will bring lasting joy, only to find we need even more to feel that thrill again. It's like running on a treadmill—no matter how fast you go, you end up in the same emotional spot.

DIGGING DEEPER

Write your answers to the following journaling prompts.

Recognizing The Hedonic Treadmill

In what areas of my life do I find myself constantly seeking more (e.g., possessions, achievements, experiences), and how often do these things deliver lasting fulfillment?

How does the excitement of getting something new or achieving a goal fade over time? What emotions do I experience when the thrill wears off?

Getting Off The Treadmill

What values or goals are truly important to me? How can I pursue them in a way that aligns with my deeper sense of purpose, rather than simply chasing fleeting pleasure?

Aligning Goals with True Values

How can I refocus my energy on experiences or achievements that contribute to my personal growth and well-being, rather than just accumulating material things?

_____

_____

_____

_____

_____

_____

_____

_____

_____

_____

_____

_____

_____

_____

_____

Chapter 11

DREAMS DEFERRED

Sometimes, what we desire may not be possible, and we might be clinging to dreams that have long since expired, holding our happiness hostage. They say deferred dreams make the heart sick, and this rings true. There's a grieving process that occurs when a dream doesn't materialize.

DIGGING DEEPER

Write your answers to the following journaling prompts.

Reflecting on Old Dreams

What are some dreams or goals that I've been holding onto for a long time that no longer seem possible or aligned with my life today? How do these unfulfilled dreams make me feel?

Letting Go and Symbolic Release

In what way can I symbolically release these old dreams, such as writing them down and letting them go, burning them, or burying something that represents them?

Moving Forward with New Goals

What are new dreams or goals that excite me and feel more aligned with who I am today?

Embracing the Future

How can I embrace the process of moving forward, knowing that it's okay to change direction and release things that no longer serve me?

_____

_____

_____

_____

_____

_____

_____

_____

_____

_____

_____

_____

_____

_____

_____

_____

Chapter 12

NEGATIVE EXPERIENCES

Life is filled with both positive and negative experiences, but our brains often amplify the negative to keep us safe. This focus on negativity, called the "negativity bias," can lead us to remember bad experiences more vividly than the good ones, making it essential to examine the narratives we create around our experiences. I often ask clients, "Is the narrative I'm telling myself accurate, and is it helpful?" Many discover their narratives aren't entirely accurate, and even if they are, they may not serve the life they want.

DIGGING DEEPER

Write your answers to the following journaling prompts.

Reflecting on Your Current Narrative

How do I typically frame my life experiences—do I focus more on the positive or negative aspects? How might negativity bias influence the way I remember and react to past events?

Questioning the Accuracy of Your Narrative

How have my past experiences, including patterns of negativity or self-doubt, shaped my current mindset, and what positive aspects or hidden lessons might I be overlooking in the difficult moments?

How does the current narrative I tell myself support or hinder my long-term goals and values?

Reframing for Growth and Alignment

How can I shift my thinking to focus on the progress I've made, rather than only on what went wrong or what I haven't achieved yet?

_____

_____

_____

_____

_____

_____

_____

_____

_____

_____

_____

_____

_____

_____

_____

_____

Chapter 13

COMPARISON

Comparison is truly a thief of joy. While it's a central theme of this book, it also deserves its own spotlight. Comparison not only robs us of happiness, but it can also turn us into people who will do anything to get ahead. Learning to stop comparing ourselves is key to finding happiness and fulfilling our purpose.

DIGGING DEEPER

Write your answers to the following journaling prompts.

Identifying Your Strengths and Talents

What qualities do I tend to downplay or overlook, and how can exploring personality tests, feedback from others, or examples from the web help me better recognize and value my unique gifts?

Shifting the Focus Away from Comparison

When I find myself comparing, what specific qualities or accomplishments in others am I focusing on, and how can I shift my attention to my own strengths and uniqueness to embrace my individuality?

What actions can I take to use my gifts to create a positive impact, rather than feeling inadequate in comparison to others?

Reinforcing Your Personal Value

How can I celebrate my achievements and qualities, no matter how small, to counteract the negative effects of comparison?

Chapter 14

THOUGHT DISTORTIONS

Thought distortions are maladaptive ways the brain interprets information that have negative impacts on our lives over time. Many of these distortions can lead to common mental health disorders, such as depression and anxiety, and contribute to an overall less-than-satisfactory life. Some common thought distortions that sabotage your own personal happiness include all-or-nothing thinking, catastrophizing, overgeneralization, over-personalization, and emotional reasoning.

DIGGING DEEPER

Write your answers to the following journaling prompts.

Identifying Common Thought Distortions

Which of these common thought distortion patterns do I recognize in my thinking? How can I become more aware of these thought distortions when they occur in my thinking?

- All-or-nothing thinking: seeing things as either completely good or completely bad.

- Catastrophizing: imagining the worst possible outcome.

- Overgeneralization: making broad conclusions based on one event.

- Over-personalization: taking responsibility for things that are outside of your control.

- Emotional reasoning: assuming your negative emotions reflect objective reality.

- Negativity bias: noticing all of the negatives, while ignoring the positives

Examining the Impact of Thought Distortions

How are these thought patterns affecting my mood, behaviors, or relationships? Do I notice any patterns of negative thinking that lead to stress, anxiety, or depression?

Challenging Thought Distortions

How can I reframe my thoughts when I catch myself engaging in a thought distortion?

Seeking Support

If these thought distortions are having a significant negative impact on my life, how open am I to seeking therapy or other support to address them?

_____

_____

_____

_____

_____

_____

_____

Chapter 15

THE NEED TO CONTROL

A major source of unhappiness is not understanding the boundaries of what we can control and what we cannot. Our need to control things and people outside ourselves increases anxiety, frustration, and anger once we inevitably run into the fact that we cannot control certain things. Control is a fear response. We attempt to control when we are afraid of something.

DIGGING DEEPER
Write your answers to the following journaling prompts.

Recognizing Your Need for Control
What are some situations, people, or outcomes I try to control that are beyond my power, and how do I feel when I realize I can't control them (e.g., anxiety, frustration, anger, or fear)?

Exploring the Underlying Fears
What fears might be driving my need to control certain things? For example, fear of failure, rejection, uncertainty, or loss?

Releasing the Need for Control
What aspects of a situation or relationship can I control, and how might accepting what I cannot control reduce my stress and improve my well-being?

What practices (e.g., mindfulness, meditation/prayer, or journaling) can help me let go of control and focus on what I can manage?

_____

_____

_____

_____

_____

_____

_____

_____

_____

_____

_____

_____

_____

_____

_____

_____

Chapter 16

LACK OF DISCIPLINE

Most people cringe at the word "discipline" because it often brings up feelings of failure. Ask someone where they lack discipline, and they'll quickly have an answer. So how can we improve? The key steps are finding your "why," getting accountability, and taking small, manageable steps.

DIGGING DEEPER
Write your answers to the following journaling prompts.

Identifying Areas for Improvement
What are the areas in my life where I want to be more disciplined (e.g., health, finances, relationships, work, personal growth)?

Discovering Your "Why"
What is my deeper motivation for being disciplined, and how can I make my "why" visible, like through reminders or vision boards?

Taking Small Steps
What small, manageable steps can I take to build discipline in each area, and what potential obstacles might I face, along with ways to prepare to overcome them?

Celebrating "wins"

How will I track my progress and celebrate small victories along the way?

_____

_____

_____

_____

_____

_____

_____

_____

_____

_____

_____

_____

_____

_____

_____

_____

Chapter 17

LACK OF SOCIAL SUPPORT

A major issue in our society is the increasing disconnection we feel from others. Humans are social creatures, and despite this, we are becoming increasingly isolated from each other. This is wreaking havoc on our mental health, especially as it relates to how human contact actually helps us cope with life's difficulties. Having little support and feeling isolated makes life much harder to handle.

DIGGING DEEPER

Write your answers to the following journaling prompts.

Assessing Your Current Support System

Who are the people I currently consider part of my support system? How often do you actively make time for, and connect with your support system?

Identifying Areas for Improvement

Are there opportunities to expand my support network, and how can I challenge beliefs like "I don't like people" or "People will judge me"?

Overcoming Barriers to Connection

What barriers prevent me from experiencing a stronger support system, and how can I address these barriers?

Rebuilding Connection

What small, actionable steps can I take this week to reconnect with someone I care about or to build a new connection?

_____

_____

_____

_____

_____

_____

_____

_____

_____

_____

_____

_____

_____

_____

_____

_____

Chapter 18

COMFORT ZONES

We live in a society that prioritizes convenience and comfort. Need a quick meal? Microwave it. Want to shop? Amazon delivers. Looking for love? Just swipe left. Even our cars keep us perfectly warm. While we can easily access many things, true value often requires stepping outside our comfort zones.

The brain craves comfort and familiarity, making it easy to become "comfortable" in negative situations. Learning to push past discomfort is crucial for a fulfilling life.

DIGGING DEEPER

Write your answers to the following journaling prompts.

Counting the Cost of being Comfortable

How has staying in my comfort zone in certain areas impacted my life? Am I missing out on opportunities, growth, or deeper connections?

Stepping Outside the Comfort Zone

What is one challenge I can take on to step outside of my comfort zone in an area where I want to grow?

How will I know when I'm making progress, and how can I celebrate small victories along the way?

Long Term Gains

How might stepping out of my comfort zone improve my life in the long term and how have you benefited in the past from pushing through discomfort? Can you use those experiences to motivate yourself now?

_____

_____

_____

_____

_____

_____

_____

_____

_____

_____

_____

_____

_____

_____

_____

Chapter 19

LACK OF SELF-CARE

Lack of self-care is one reason we may not be feeling an overall sense of well-being. Self-care does not have to be extravagant. Spa days and vacations aren't the only way to take care of ourselves. Self-care could look like taking a lunch during the day instead of foregoing it to get more work done. Or making sure you are getting enough rest at night instead of doom-scrolling on social media. Or making sure you are scheduling doctor appointments for yourself. Self-care doesn't always mean expensive; it means checking in with yourself and getting your needs met.

DIGGING DEEPER

Write your answers to the following journaling prompts.

Identifying Gaps in Self-Care

What basic needs am I neglecting, and what self-care practices can I introduce to manage feelings of overwhelm or burnout?

Planning for Better Self-Care Practices

What simple, daily actions can I take to prioritize self-care (e.g., setting aside time for a hobby, preparing healthy meals, or going for a walk)?

What boundaries do I need to set to make time for self-care, whether at work, in relationships, or with social media?

Overcoming Barriers

How can I reframe self-care as a necessary investment in my well-being rather than a luxury or indulgence?

_____

_____

_____

_____

_____

_____

_____

_____

_____

_____

_____

_____

_____

_____

Chapter 20

MONEY

While making money doesn't significantly boost happiness beyond a certain point, lacking enough for basic needs and some wants can negatively affect your mood. It's easy to say that money doesn't bring happiness, but it's out of touch with reality to say money doesn't matter at all.

Reflect on ways you might have unintentionally belittled someone struggling financially by encouraging them to "just try harder." Similarly, consider how you may have downplayed your own accomplishments by comparing yourself to those with more.

DIGGING DEEPER

Write your answers to the following journaling prompts.

Reflecting on Attitudes Toward Money

How do I currently view money and its role in my life? Do I see it as a tool, a source of stress, or something else?

Shifting Mindset Toward Compassion

How can you show compassion to others who are financially struggling without oversimplifying their situation, and what does practicing financial compassion for yourself look like?

Reducing Financial Comparison and Building Gratitude

In what ways have I fallen into the trap of comparing my financial situation to others? How does this affect my happiness and sense of self-worth?

Taking Positive Action

How can I set realistic financial goals aligned with my values, and what manageable steps can I take to educate myself about money management to improve my financial well-being?

_____

_____

_____

_____

_____

_____

_____

_____

_____

_____

_____

_____

_____

Chapter 21

GRATITUDE

Practicing gratitude has been found to be one of the most effective and least expensive ways to find joy in our lives right now. Gratitude helps you step off the hedonic treadmill, allowing feelings of comparison, envy, and jealousy to lose their grip. It is difficult to stay envious if you are consistently being grateful. It is a choice that we have to intentionally make daily.

DIGGING DEEPER

Write your answers to the following journaling prompts.

Morning Gratitude Practice

Before engaging with your phone first thing in the morning, what are three things I am truly grateful for as I begin my day? Reflect on small or big moments, relationships, or opportunities.

Reflecting on Gratitude Throughout the Day

What are three things I appreciated about yesterday? How do you feel when you reflect on the moments you are grateful for?

Deepening Your Gratitude Practice

How can pausing to feel grateful for overlooked parts of my life, such as routines or basic needs, help reduce feelings of envy, comparison, or negativity?

How can I create reminders throughout the day to keep gratitude top of mind?

Chapter 22

KINDNESS

I help clients improve their lives by encouraging them to build a bank of positive experiences. By investing in this bank, you create a reserve of positive emotions to balance out negative experiences. One effective way to make deposits is through acts of kindness. In our busy lives, we often overlook kindness, but it significantly boosts our mood.

DIGGING DEEPER

Write your answers to the following journaling prompts.

Planning Acts of Kindness
What are some small, meaningful acts of kindness I can perform today? Consider gestures for strangers, friends, family, or coworkers.

Noticing Patterns and Growth
Are there specific types of kind acts that resonate with me more or feel especially rewarding? Was there a shift in your mood after these acts of kindess?

Expanding Acts of Kindness
How can I cultivate kindness toward myself, ensuring I include self-care in my "bank" of positive experiences?

What acts of kindness can I plan for tomorrow or the coming week to continue building my bank of positive experiences?

_____

_____

_____

_____

_____

_____

_____

_____

_____

_____

_____

_____

_____

_____

_____

Chapter 23

STAY TRUE TO YOU

Many people get caught up in trying to keep up with societal norms, forgetting that we are all unique individuals. In our quest to fit in, we often judge ourselves based on how well we are able to conform to what society says we should be instead of valuing our own uniqueness. Until we embrace our authenticity, we'll continue to struggle with comparison and envy. Recognizing the importance that our own uniqueness brings to the world is key to escaping the comparison trap.

DIGGING DEEPER
Write your answers to the following journaling prompts.

Reflecting on Compromise
How often do I find myself agreeing with others or going along with societal expectations to avoid conflict or fit in?

What are some core values or beliefs that define who I am? How often do I honor these in my daily life?

Building Authenticity
What steps can I take this week to live more authentically and focus on what truly matters to me, even when faced with external pressure?

What practices or affirmations can help me reconnect with my authentic self when I feel the urge to compare myself to others?

Chapter 24

YOU VS. YOU

The term "you vs. you" highlights that our only true competition is with ourselves, not others. While everyone compares from time to time, some people regularly speak and think self-deprecating comments like, "If I had your body," or "If my husband was like that." But what if you removed the limitations on your own body, career, and relationships?

DIGGING DEEPER
Write your answers to the following journaling prompts.

Recognizing Limiting Beliefs
In what areas of my life do I feel like I'm falling short compared to others (e.g., career, relationships, appearance) and how do these comparisons hold me back or make me feel "not enough"?

Releasing Limiting Beliefs
What evidence do I have that contradicts these old beliefs?

What do I appreciate about my body, career, relationships, and other areas of my life right now?

Building a "You Vs. You" Mindset
How can I track and celebrate progress in my life without comparing it to someone else's journey?

Chapter 25

DELAYED GRATIFICATION

Countless studies have been done to prove that the delaying of gratification leads to more long-term satisfaction. It is our need for instant gratification that gets in the way of what we truly want. If you are going to be successful long-term at anything, you will have to learn the art of delaying gratification.

DIGGING DEEPER

Write your answers to the following journaling prompts.

Recognizing Instant Gratification

In which areas of your life do you tend to seek instant gratification (e.g., eating, spending money, entertainment), and how does instant gratification impact your long-term goals and progress?

Evaluating Goals

What benefits have I experienced when you successfully delayed gratification in the past?

Strategies for Delaying Gratification

What are 1-3 concrete actions you can take to delay gratification for the next four weeks in order to achieve your goals?

What distractions or temptations prevent me from delaying gratification, and how can I overcome them by setting milestones to stay motivated and celebrate small successes?

Chapter 26

EMOTIONS ARE OUR GPS - PART 1

We were all taught different things about our emotions growing up. How these beliefs were formed in childhood can impact how we navigate our emotions and relationships as adults. Did you grow up in a family that made emotions ok, or did you grow up in a family that taught you that pushing down emotions was best?

DIGGING DEEPER

Write your answers to the following journaling prompts.

Reflecting on Your Family's Emotional Climate

How were emotions expressed in my family growing up? Were emotions seen as positive or negative, and how were they treated?

What phrases or behaviors in my family influenced how I understand and manage my emotions today (e.g., "Big girls don't cry," "Be tough," "Don't let them see you upset")?

In what ways do I find myself repeating emotional patterns from my childhood in my current relationships?

Exploring Emotional Freedom

How can I start expressing my emotions more authentically and healthily, both to myself and others?

Chapter 26

EMOTIONS ARE OUR GPS - PART 2

Most of us spend a great amount of time trying to ignore and avoid emotions. Especially ones that we consider "negative." The truth is emotions in and of themselves are neither positive nor negative. They are just an experience. They are neutral. Each emotion has a different job of telling us what is going on at a deeper level. It connects us to this earth experience we are all having. Without emotions, life is dull.

DIGGING DEEPER
Write your answers to the following journaling prompts.

Exploring Current Emotional Expression
How do I typically respond to emotions, especially those you consider negative or unacceptable? Do you tend to suppress or avoid emotions?

What emotions do you find most challenging to experience or express?

Challenging Old Mindsets
What positive impact could processing your emotions have on your life and relationships?

How can you create space for yourself to experience and understand my emotions without judgment, and begin to process them more effectively today?

Chapter 27

MAKE A PLAN

Many of us have heard the quote, "If you fail to plan, then you plan to fail." So much of what we want to accomplish doesn't fail because we can't do it, but because we don't know what to do or fail to plan out how we will do it. In order to reach our goals in life we must be clear about what they are, have a plan, and consistently work the plan. Writing down our visions is a necessary step in living the life we want.

DIGGING DEEPER

Write your answers to the following journaling prompts.

Clarifying Your Goals:

What are two goals you want to work on right now? Why are these important to you?

How will you know when you have reached your goal and how do you envision your life changing once you achieve these goals?

Planning For Success

How can I break down each goal into smaller, manageable steps, and when will I start? What strategies will I use to hold myself accountable?

Staying Consistent

How can you track your progress and make your goal-setting process more enjoyable or rewarding?

Chapter 28

PRACTICE

Anytime we are starting something new, it takes practice to perfect it. Practicing good habits has to be intentional at first because you have been practicing the not-so-good habits for a while. After a while of practicing the new habit the brain will eventually catch on and turn the new habit into being on autopilot just like the old habit. The most important thing about creating a new habit is not giving up in the hardest stage, which is typically once the emotion of excitement has worn off and motivation wanes. We have to learn to push past this stage in order to make the new habit stick.

DIGGING DEEPER

Write your answers to the following journaling prompts.

Choosing Better Habits

What is one habit you want to create? (e.g., being more grateful, exercising regularly, eating healthier, etc.)? Why do you want to develop this habit?

Building and Maintaining Better Habits

What specific actions will I take each day to build this new habit, and how can I create reminders to stay consistent?

What strategies can you use to push through the tough moments when you feel like giving up?

Celebrating Progress

How will you track your progress with this habit (e.g., journaling, a habit tracker, setting milestones), and how will you celebrate staying consistent along the way.

_____

_____

_____

_____

_____

_____

_____

_____

_____

_____

_____

_____

_____

_____

_____

_____

_____

Chapter 29

MINDFULNESS

Mindfulness is the intentional act of staying in the present moment. Most people spend most of the time with their mind wandering to either the past or the future. Being mindful is connected to many positive outcomes, including improved mental, spiritual and physical health. People often get frustrated that they can't keep their mind from wandering, however, the mind has to be trained to stay in the present moment, especially with living in a world of constant distraction.

DIGGING DEEPER
Write your answers to the following journaling prompts.

Practicing Mindfulness
Using the habit that you wrote down from Chapter 28, how can you incorporate mindfulness into that habit? (e.g., when exercising, be aware of how your body feels; when practicing gratitude, focus on the present moment of the things you are thankful for)

When you notice your mind wandering, how will you gently bring it back to the present moment to stay connected to your habit?

Celebrating Progress
How can you celebrate small victories, especially when you catch yourself returning to the present moment?

At the end of each week, reflect on how being mindful has impacted your progress in forming your new habit.

Chapter 30

SAVORING

Savoring is the use of thoughts and actions to increase the intensity, duration, and appreciation of positive experiences and emotions. Savoring is the act of completely enjoying an experience. It's noticing the sounds of a body of water, the smell of the pine trees. It is fully enjoying the taste of your coffee instead of just gulping it down on the way out of the door. Most of the time, when doing an activity, we are partly distracted from the enjoyment of the activity and not being fully present in the moment. By fully engaging with the present moment and savoring the experience, you may find that the positive emotions last longer and feel more fulfilling.

DIGGING DEEPER

Write your answers to the following journaling prompts.

Savoring Experiences

What is an experience you would like to savor (e.g., a walk in nature, a meal, a conversation, or time spent with loved ones)?

How can you engage all five senses to fully immerse yourself in this experience? Think about:

- Sight: What do you see around you? What colors, shapes, or patterns stand out?

- Sound: What sounds surround you? Are there any specific sounds that enhance the experience (e.g., birds chirping, waves crashing)?

- Smell: What smells do you notice? How does the scent contribute to your enjoyment?

- Taste: If relevant, what flavors are you experiencing? How do they enhance the moment?

- Touch: How do the textures and sensations feel? Can you feel the warmth of the sun, the softness of a fabric, or the coolness of a breeze?

Expanding on Savoring Experiences

As you savor the experience, how does it make you feel emotionally? Are you feeling peaceful, joyful, grateful, or any other emotion?

How can you incorporate savoring into other parts of your daily life to increase appreciation and joy?

_____

_____

_____

_____

_____

_____

_____

_____

_____

Chapter 31

FINDING PURPOSE

A key part of moving away from comparison and finding joy in your own life is discovering work or a purpose that brings you fulfillment. While the meaning of life is a deep topic, research shows that having a sense of purpose boosts happiness. Purpose happens when your talents, passions, and desire to help others align with real opportunities.

DIGGING DEEPER
Write your answers to the following journaling prompts.

Identify Your Gifts and Talents
What are your natural strengths or abilities? Consider talents that come easily to you or things that others often compliment you on. Feel free to google strengths and abilities if you can't think of anything.

Using Your Gifts and Talents to Serve Others
Is there a specific area where you feel passionate about helping (e.g., supporting others in their mental health, using creativity to help children, or organizing events for a cause)?

Think of a time when you felt truly fulfilled, purposeful, or like you were "in flow." What were you doing? Who were you helping? How did you feel during and after that experience?

Pursue Your Purpose

Write down a plan to take action and use your gifts. Whether it's starting a side project, volunteering, or having more meaningful conversations, make steps toward aligning your daily actions with your sense of purpose.

_____

_____

_____

_____

_____

_____

_____

_____

_____

_____

_____

_____

_____

_____

_____

_____

Chapter 32

CONSISTENCY

When we neglect what we know we should do, we pay the price with our self-respect and self-esteem. Consistency in reaching our goals brings a sense of achievement that no one can take from us. With all the information available today, the challenge isn't knowing what to do—it's applying it. Often, it's not a lack of talent or opportunity holding us back—it's a lack of consistency.

DIGGING DEEPER
Write your answers to the following journaling prompts.

Identifying Areas for Consistency
What area in your life do you feel could benefit from more consistency (e.g., health, career, relationships)?

Setting Achievable Goals and Knowing Your "Why."
With a goal or habit you have chosen from previous chapters remind yourself why you chose this goal. What is the long-term benefit of achieving it consistently?

Make A Plan To Make it Stick
What is the action plan and what challenges are you facing in being consistent with this goal? How can you plan differently to handle them more effectively?

How can you remind yourself of the value and importance of this goal, especially on days when it's difficult?

Chapter 33

VISUALIZE

The mind is incredible. When we visualize something, it's like speaking the brain's language, it starts aligning everything to make that vision happen. Ever seen an ad for food, and suddenly you can't stop thinking about it? That's visualization at work. TV, after all, is "tell-a-vision." It is designed to plant images in your mind that motivate you to follow through with whatever action the advertiser intends.

DIGGING DEEPER

Write your answers to the following journaling prompts.

Create a Vision

Take a few minutes to close your eyes and visualize yourself achieving your goal. What does success look like for you? Describe the scene in detail. What do you hear, see, taste, and smell in the moment of success, and what physical sensations do you experience in your body?

Write about the emotions you would feel upon achieving your goal. How would you celebrate your success?

Make a Plan

After visualizing your goal, what action steps can you take in the next 24 hours to move closer to that vision? Write down specific steps and set a time frame.

Avoiding distractions

How will you deal with distractions, setbacks, and negativity from others as you pursue your vision?

Congratulations

on finishing your workbook! Keep applying these principles, and **stay present, consistent, and *grateful*.** And remember, stay out of your neighbor's yard!